HOSTAGE

New & Selected Poems

Hostage

New & Selected Poems

Emily Fragos

The Sheep Meadow Press
Rhinebeck, New York

Copyright © 2011 by Emily Fragos

All rights reserved. No part of this publication may be reproduced or transmitted in any form or by any means, electronic or mechanical, including photocopy, recording, or any information storage and retrieval system, without permission in writing from the publisher, except in the case of brief quotations in reviews.

Designed and typeset by The Sheep Meadow Press.
Distributed by The University Press of New England.

All inquiries and permission requests should be addressed to the publisher:

The Sheep Meadow Press
PO Box 1345
Riverdale, NY 10471

Library of Congress Cataloging-in-Publication Data

Fragos, Emily.
  Hostage : new & selected poems / Emily Fragos.
     p. cm.
  ISBN 978-1-931357-93-7 (alk. paper)
  I. Title.
  PS3606.R345H67 2011
  811'.6--dc22

                                2011001388

Cover Art: Francisco Goya: *The Dog*, c. 1819-1823, Museo del Prado, Madrid.

FOR MICHELE, CHRISTINE & STEFAN

Contents

I

Nemesis	7
To Pavese	8
Bach Fugue	10
Horsehead at a Parisian Fair	11
A Tapestry of Père Bourgeois	12
Kyrie	13
19 Chopin Waltzes	14
Beast of Burden	15
Kafka's Sister	16
The Actor	17
The Child, Joseph Cornell	18
Little Mercutios	19
Away	20

II

Little O, Earth	23
Spindlers	24
Must	25
The Lake	26
For Helen, My Sister	27
Silent Movie	28
The Juggler's Hands	29
To the Knee	30
The Last Circus on Earth	31
Hereafter	32
Insomnia	33
Fortune	34

Balanchine's Male Dancers	35
Into Great Silence	36

III

The Blind are Sleeping	39
Chopiniana	40
for Kaspar Hauser	41
Winter Carnival in a Small Flemish Town	42
Quartet for the End of Time	43
For Them	44
Winter Gigue	45
Divertissement	46
Muses	47
Asbury Park	48
Art Brut	49
Figure with Hat	50
The Cellar	51
On Forgetting	52

IV

Hostage	55
An Old Illness	56
Notre Dame de Paris	57
Lazarus, Come Out	58
Anacreon	59
Suzanne Farrell, *Davidsbündlertänze*	60
Hibernation	61
Metanoia	62
Middle World	63

God of Sleep	64
To Balanchine	65
[Exit, Pursued by a Bear.	66
Chernobyl	67

Selected Poems from *Little Savage*

A Note on Emily Fragos's *Little Savage* by Richard Howard	71
Apollo's Kiss	75
Mondays	76
Medieval	77
Glenn Gould, Dead at 50	78
Graces	79
The Art of the Insane	80
Logic	81
Visitations, but None Come	83
Host	84
While You Slept	85
Cri de Coeur	86
The Path	87
The Drowned	88
Company	89
In the Egyptian Museum	90
In Memoriam	91
Sorrow	92
Hall of Records	94
Increase of Appetite	95
The Scarlatti Sun	97
Notes	101

Acknowledgments

The author wishes to thank the editors of the following publications where these poems originally appeared, sometimes in slightly different versions.

The American Poetry Review: "*Lazarus, Come Out*," "Metanoia," "Silent Movie," "To Pavese"

Barrow Street: "Spindlers," "To Balanchine"

The Boston Review: "Chernobyl"

The Cimarron Review: "Insomnia," "19 Chopin Waltzes"

Columbia: Journal of Literature & Art: "An Old Illness," "The Blind Are Sleeping," "Chopiniana"

The New Yorker: "Bach Fugue"

Ploughshares: "Hostage," "Muses"

Poetry: "Nemesis," "The Cellar"

The Threepenny Review: "The Juggler's Hands"

The Yale Review: "Little Mercutios"

"Bach Fugue" appeared in the poetry anthology *Music's Spell*, published by Everyman's Pocket Library.

"Suzanne Farrell, *Davidsbündlertänze*" appeared in the poetry anthology *The Dance*, published by Everyman's Pocket Library.

"19 Chopin Waltzes" and "Chopiniana" appeared in the poetry anthology *Chopin with Cherries*, published by Moonrise Press.

"Nemesis," "19 Chopin Waltzes" and "The Cellar" were reprinted in *Verse Daily*.

"Nemesis" was reprinted in *The Columbia Granger's World of Poetry*.

HOSTAGE

Just being here
I am here
and the snow falls.
                    —Issa

I

Nemesis

The old men with too much gamble in them, whose eyes

Are at peace only when all is lost, see the Queen's quiet face

On the deck of cards, the red cuff of her cloak, the raw tip

Of her tongue, the blood on her dress…What fled from them

In their frenzies comes tiptoeing back, choiring, to the marble

Concert hall where Nemesis, in velvet opera cape, is beginning

Her recitative: *it is your turn to go slowly now, with hands*

clasped behind your back, drowsy from the earth's sweet

abundance and her great deprivations, the rows of crooked trees,

the streets' bright monotony, to gather up the starving…

To Pavese

The city will appear before you
as otherworldly, inviting only
to those who suffer.

The dog tethered to the pole
stares at forms that move
with such muscle, ease. No thoughts
impede their shapes. There is kindness still
and what tenderness remains
for the crazed,
the rain brings out.

The classmate, so lithe, you followed
to the bookstore, to watch in secret,
and the arab who invited you to the café
and failed to show up,
you in your velvet pants, Cesare, stunned
to be rejected by one who is no one,
are long gone.

Through the giant eye of the telescope,
they have sighted
the end of the beginning,
radiating galaxies
of deep fire, something
finally different
to tell you.

And the Coliseum cats
still come out at night.
They have become as famous as you
for being ruined and suspicious.
They grow vicious, you know,
captured in giant nets,
hissing and spitting.

Bach Fugue

Frees the horses from their mechanical bolts,

Keeps the fire from spreading to the sleepers' floor.

The miming dancers in the wings (*swell to great*)

Begin their sly whisperings, their tired arms

Around each other's waist. The old woman spoons yellow cake

Into her (*celestial tremulous*) mouth. Is capable of putting

Poor Gloucester's eyes, glistening, back. Catches the jumpers

With invisible nets from their sad, night bridges;

Finds all those who have been lost to you. The great

Chords, once struck, can never decay.

Horsehead at a Parisian Fair

You are still in your face
Where the sun warms your mouth that once bit a mare's
In death-defying pursuit
In the memory of your standing, your fetlocks
Flecked with gold and white
At the flies that arrive full force to gnaw on you
You could almost toss your mane
Much as you would like to move, you look back at everything
In your path with glassy eyes, the mind of the quadriplegic
And of all that is captive
When you died, they placed you on your side
And bent your legs for running

A Tapestry of Pere Bourgeois

Young girl, all grudge-mouth, with the soul of an old man
in smock and heavy shoes, clutches at the stringy ankle

of a woman with leaking breasts. The mother's milk
drips to the floor, helping no one. In another room,

her father's fabric garden: moths flutter by silver filament;
soft children and white horses at rest; a favorite spiral road

where corpulent friars and nuns eternally process, arriving
at the turn, joyful by the swing of their arms, in the land of plague.

One slave, who can go no farther, carrying the spoiled mistress
in her coach-basket through the narrowest alps passes,

has the hardship faded out of his blurry face and breathes
through centuries and a red-thread mouth. Hoisted high,

the impossible one munches on kringles with sugar
and cream, while fierce cats slink to lap up the sweets.

Kyrie

The goal posts are off-kilter and the moon slides into my shoes.
I could disappear into the night like a hitcher,
Firebird of cinders,
Lost dogs, rising from their urine-soaked bedding
To await their human names.

In the dark cells, Beato Angelico's angels stream,
Spirals of pure solace, iodine weavings;
And the shining bodies draped in cloth,
Hands and feet missing, are
Feeling the dance in their mouths.

19 Chopin Waltzes

Snow falls from rafters of pink, swollen clouds;
moonlight drenches the peasants' fields.

The feathered flesh of a fish, the juice of a peach,
the silver rivers before we named them with color.

All the begetting: the weak limbs and soft bellies,
the faces elongated like the devil himself. The devil

himself! The ship that sails to dreams of Achilles,
the palace of the deaf, the murmuring in centuries' rooms,

the crying of turtle doves, the fleet-footed dancing.
On Earth as in heaven, beauty without reason.

Beast of Burden

piled so high the legs buckle
hit with a thin stick whistled at
shouted at kicked with their heels

end me
on this earth with these humans
under a boiling sun in a world of rocks

remove the tower of wooden collar
studded with bells
from round my thick neck
so that removed
from all halters I may wander

let the dust blow me away
to long quiet roads
the clip clop of my feet
the only music I hear

or let me be gently lead like the old
or pull the wooden carts of babies
and nothing more

Lord of the Ass
lay me down
unencumbered in your green pastures
for which they incessantly pray

the air cooling and petting the bones of my ears
brushing my skull
the still waters washing out
my braying mouth

Kafka's Sister

…but here is my Ottla, so alive inside her dressing gown,

her breasts like lady apples. See how she bends to pick up

Puss 'n Boots and bring him to her mouth, kissing him

on the rump! (That I were that cat!) How funny she finds me,

seated in my straight-backed chair, fastidious in overcoat,

gloves and bowler hat. "You look like you've seen a ghost,"

she is laughing. "So Franz!" Banished from my kingdom,

all icy winter and future's grief, now that she is here, her

dark hair falling down and around her face and the animal.

The Actor

There will be a test and you will fail. You must take your clothes off,
crawl, carry your dead child in your arms from there to here—pray

our Cordelia is beautiful and light to lift—and when all is gone to slaughter,
die here, mark this, with her in your arms. Imagine the first Lear, with nothing

to warn him, nothing to set the pace, the good example, the comforting song.
You will fail in every important way, the directions run on; you cannot grip

this jeweled handle the way you once did, with vigor, with awesome beauty
toward your enemies. As you go, the limbs will stiffen, and pain follow you

like a mongrel cur, who has more life left in him than you. Now, howl
above the infants' squalls, the roiling oceans, the primate laughter. Now, hush;

skin of elephant, hands of wax. Weep woman's tears, chin all aquiver.
Say: my eyes broke for you. Prop master, what have we for torn stones?

The Child, Joseph Cornell

Happy to swim in and out of her private castle, the fish does not need a companion. To protect her, you buy gallant toy soldiers with muskets on their shoulders, a tiny cannon, one-inch horses with faceless riders, their feet glued to the stirrups, and enter them into the water. You marvel at how improvisational and passionate in her assorted movements your fish is. You stare unceasingly at her and begin to submerge gifts, one by one: a sleeping pink dollhead, a cat's-eye, a strand of paste pearls from your mother's jewelry box, a pocket watch with missing hands, a thimble…until, suddenly, you know, and with what a Mozartean pang of immense tenderness you know, that you will spend the rest of your life at this glittering masked ball.

Little Mercutios

She cackles like a bird, the old crow,
being fed by your mother
with a fork and a spoon,
while sentimental tunes
from another era
play softly in the background.

The little Mercutios
rub balloons to their sweaters,
stick them to their chests, squealing
and preening in the medieval square.

The cats have not missed you
as you thought they would.
They have found the sun.

The wedding party
walks slowly from the church
and the silent witnesses with hard faces
line the sides of the road.

The overwhelmed pharmacist, deaf
in one ear, whose little packages
you stole out from under him
when he turned his broad back,
is just where you left him,
hunched over his insoluble papers,
his crates of white lotion.

The sad soldiers are coming home.

Away

The faint, hoarse breathing of a near-ghost sliding her arms

into a coat's listless sleeves. Just where does she think she is going in

that mothy thing, with a filthy stray shoved into a pocket, mumbling,

casting elephant shadows along the black walls of blind alleys,

crumbling buildings, a padlocked lumber yard, the dump,

and farther out, the red-lit hut with psychic inside, until

where, on the edge of the dark city, nothing more is.

II

Little O, Earth

Feeling your body move over the earth
where winged things flutter
at the base of the tree—give us

the high held note; the grace of the pasture animal,
unperturbed, its eloquent eyes,
the taste of dirt and grass in its mouth,

the yoke, the brand, the butcher's block
not part of its mind; the gaiety of a small bird
or a blue field flower, alone or together with others,

swaying. Take us, not with derision,
but with the folly of adoration
for the odd nature of us.

Spindlers

Turn, she hums, and her silver pail fills

With fish of snipped cloth.

Filament goes in and out of the primitive eye, is cut

By Atropos's blades. Vestments must be stitched to fit,

Cinched at the thickening waist, bodice, hips.

Clotho's hands quiver at the choosing. Lachesis burns like ice.

One good lengthening pull and the stalwart body reforms

To limp, bulge, curve, hole. Spinning by dark, they ruin

Their eyes. The sisters have no use for words.

Must

for my mother

I

In the garden, you are scolding phantom children. Your hands
are dry as wood. A tree with its roots, its leaves—the living parts—

leans awkwardly away from you. The birds lift from their sticks
and vanish with their secret faces. The garden wall is growing darker,

quieter, deepening into the ground. There is no way round it. We are
come to the door that when pushed, shoulder-shoved, will not give.

II

You have caught everything, the whitish-man
whispers in your ear. Your pale face is clean now of harm and humiliation

at the hands of the throng. You must leave the tree to its branch songs
and the ravishment of the music to the first birds. Leave for the last time

your gifts at the doors of friends while they sleep. River, enter your mouth,
your bones, turn you in your sleep. Let the flood come, the little fishes eat.

The Lake

Anguish has taken wing, dispelled is darkness, for there is no gloom where now there was distress. These words from his childhood, mysteriously summoned up, offer no solace to the fisherman who found the body in his favorite lake. We will not watch the television that allows the liars to lie, he says to his baffled wife, and begins to write his confessions on pieces of paper, burying them in the soft backyard with the dog and the birds turned to bones whose tiny skulls he kissed. He had plans to carve his failing father a walking stick from the pasture's great oak, but that is not possible.

For Helen, My Sister

The sun shines on your hospital-white gown and your bare feet.
The ground beneath you is bone-dry and filled with rocks. You pay no mind.

All the wounds have healed, the rages calmed and inconsequential
In this bright light of summer. The fatal moments of terror,

The noise of the crowd pressing close to see you, to fork round your high,
Supple body, do not disturb your gravity. It has taken so long

For your clenched fist to open, and now it is hugely bloomed,
Its fingers pointing to the hidden floor where children are filing through

In silent commotion. They could be going to the cool, sparkling
Horse's Spring, for all they know, each holding the shoulder of the next,

A tiny train of shy, amazed souls, their bare feet like yours
Not making a sound. You call out to them, in words newly minted.

Silent Movie

Suddenly all the pedestrians and street vendors

are actors in a new silent movie: *The Horse that Stole*

Our Hearts and Galloped Off the Cliff, Its Iron Hooves

Pawing. Quickly, by the North Gate, for the city

is in flames and we will all perish! The horses are pulled

by ropes round their necks. The old grip tree trunks.

The newly arrived from dung-filled lands are grabbing up

cheap wool gloves, rubber boots, golden doorknobs

and going with hands clenched. Gap-toothed women

squeeze every cherry in the box with swift, nimble fingers.

The Juggler's Hands

The poem is written in Portuguese, a language of which
I have no knowledge, and I read it while my friend prepares
eggplant and paprika soup. The dumb messenger boy has run
his donkey cart off the road and scrambled down the muddy ravine
to retrieve it. The village children, covered in muck, rummage
through his backpack and run off with the *yes* letter. The huts
are lit with torches. The one-legged man is being beaten with a log,
while thieves sneak into the tomb to sever the juggler's hands.
It is the tempest that brings the words. Take the foolish ones
to the maze, for the Master is bored. Wild ducks are hanging
in the marketplace, a delicacy for the lady on her pedestal. She has invited
the artist to paint her with her greyhounds and dwarves, the mute seamstress
altering for hours on end her taffeta and brocade. She is small-bosomed
and tight about the lips, a complainer by nature, as all unhappy people are.

To The Knee

What the surgeon put into you, severing your bones with a saw—
Crude imagining—and cementing that metallic hinge inside your pale

Skin is an affront to beauty, your peaceful exuberance, your smooth
Laughter. You would like, I know full well, to kneel, leap, stretch out

And bow in the way you were created, but pain is everywhere,
Behind and beneath you, at each side of you and splitting. It cannot be

Contained. The Greek Side is taking over and what was once a curious
Drawing in a large-sized picture book has now come to life: flesh-eating

Birds, wounding with their rapacious beaks, their brazen wings—
Ornithes Stymphalides, above my bed, grim-eyed, gawk.

The Last Circus On Earth

At the last circus on Earth, papier-mache parrots are strapped
To each child's wrist. A human elephant with a broken back, one man in front,
One in the back, makes a jaunty, grand entrance to the faint roar of the crowd.

Les Frères Mahoudeau, who have spent each entire morning mending
Their tattered tights, ballet slippers and fish net, for nothing but this matters,
Are making their tremulous way up the broken rope ladder.

The night watchman has cut loose the bear with a chained ring through its snout,
And the plumed, trick poodles, and run away with the woman who gets sawed
In half. The stuporous contortionist drowses inside the clown's yellow barrel.

Hereafter

Swords push through the unresisting
Body and the audience swoons. The pretty

Assistant in gold lamé is down below,
Eating a diet of apples (so as to squeeze

Into the slim box) and straightening her
Black seams, firing up a cherry cheroot.

There's a faint rumbling in the space above
Her. Someone's moving the contraption.

Insomnia

Here comes the sweeper of the square

With his dry, straw broom, and even the scuttling rats

And the pigeons, with their insatiable bellies,

Their ravenous mouths, have a place to go.

Every gold and crimson Mary holds her son,

Nesting, with his old man's face, thin lips and sharp nipples

On a pale chest. Even the chained lie down in the dark;

Soldiers, sick of shoveling muck and trench, dream of resting

Beneath blankets of snow. The herder grips tight the squirming

Sheep and shears it down to its pink, quivering skin.

Fortune

The stone-faced woman dares
to put herself in front of you
in a long line, knowing as the cunning
know that you will not complain,

for she has chosen you for marking.
When there was war, you survived
by being quiet, running from blows,
learning which berries were poisonous.

In this life, walking the streets of filth,
not caring if you are pounded with a pipe,
you will the frightening to stab,
the speeding to swerve, the swaying

to collapse on your head. All the bones
hold and you arrive home to the birth
of fortune: quiet fields where worked
horses are resting, the bear in the river

with a fat salmon wiggling in its mouth,
the fire that goes out before it touches
the curtain. You could lie face-down
on the pavement, so relieved are you,

as after a long cancer from which
you will never get well. You could walk
on your hands, you could prance on stilts.

Balanchine's Male Dancers

Broken-toed, Apollo-beautiful, we spoke our bones
under the weight of muse, whose each amplitudinous limb,

lifting to the rafters, proclaimed *I am it!* with your blessing.
Then, good-bye, dear, when it was our time; go in peace,

you said, leaving us hapless, unsure, tender as children
in an orphaned woods. None of us had a choice.

The cat freezes before the mouse's hole, its eyes filmed
with hunger. It was your nature to be in rapture: every lift

opening like a grief-music, every step erased with the next
until we are all hapless, vanished. Go in peace.

Into Great Silence

Most humble, they answer to the ringing of the bell
and course down the stone halls to eat together: celery broth,
baguette, pears, hard cheese. Their brown robes sail like wings

behind them. After, the old monk, hunched, climbs
the narrow stairs with a basket balanced on the precipice
of his back to feed the strays, banging on the metal dish

and calling out to them like an owl. The cats come in all their hues
and patterns to the hoo-hooing and set to the brimming food
with loud licks. The cows, sheep, and flocked birds wait for

the humans who have lost their tongues to bring seed and straw
and no fear whatsoever. There are deep prints in the overnight snow
and from a distant valley comes the echo of a peacock's squall.

If you go into town, say the orders, you must neither eat nor drink
what is graciously offered, but rest by the plain, wayside stream.
Cup your hands, brothers, and drink from the plain, wayside stream.

III

The Blind Are Sleeping

Their heads tilt gently on the pillows of the field.
Their hands, gesturing at the out-of-sight

with inexhaustible fingers, rest still as cats—
self-contained, melancholy—beside their prone masters.

The emptied body accommodates the most mottled flesh,
the most hapless limp. The blood that stops is rich

and tender. The aroma of wet grass and turf upturned
is the odor of young men, flavor of salt storm, of shout.

The sun still above is huge and boiling. The heads of the blind
warm like stones, their pale stares mesmerized, forever entering.

Their faces, unadorned, are devoid of human adoration.
Their mouths part as if they could almost sing.

Let me breathe you, says the choirmaster, who paints eyes
on their lids, and the blind who sleep—fly out.

Chopiniana

Those hermits in their caves with their violent, pleading loves,
their moist eyes, are real and understandable to me now.
Their caves are right here in the palm of my hand.

The furious world with its murmurs in white corridors,
its endless dying off, has moved into a deep, invisible room
where the occupants do nothing but stain and scratch the walls.

What remains moves fathomless and ravished, a Chopin of elation,
performing so easily what is impossible to do. I am relieved of the burden
of language and arriving and know for a fact that I need not speak.

World, I will not smile at you anymore. It is the dance in me, born—
quiver to cadence and every touch a wild tactility, the salty eye.

For Kaspar Hauser

Hopeless in suspicion, the new stray
can do nothing but bite deep into the hand

that enfolds her. She draws blood and is baffled,
cowered, to be hollered at—a child in fur and fluttering

tail. This is how my day has begun, yelling
at an animal. *Mother, I feel far from everything.*

Winter Carnival in a Small Flemish Town

On the iced-over, metal-gray pond, skaters are held
At beautiful angles by water and air. Such suppleness
Of limbs, spines, strong knees, and light, tilting heads
To balance their spinning bodies. Two boys are facing off;
One, about to touch the other's nerve, sure to bring fists
Or tears, is pulling back from the brink he'll never know.
The requisite music, a man with his lute. The selling of warm ale
In clay jugs and of spicy cakes. Under a huge, white ocean of sky,
A cow with frozen udders stands right of center, gazing past us
Like a worn-out party guest, listening to the moans of the winter dead:
Take shelter, dear people. Swathe your children, bolt your doors,
And stoke your fires. Get off that softening pond. Quick!

Quartet for the End of Time

The pianist's hands hover, await the vanishing
That will break over their heads like a flowering grief.
The tears will not be sewn together, as one by one

They fathom: I cannot care anymore, I will not miss you.
Never could they, half-mad, imagine the aloof,
The drowning, gathered inside the burying wave.

For Them

Rufus, the colored bull terrier, steps it down the cobbled streets,
accustomed to the pleasure his huge egg-shaped head brings.
Women, with their high voices, fragrant necks, and long, plaited hair,

delight him, and only once did he fear them when, a ring on one's finger,
studded with emeralds and a sharp-molded gold spiral, caught him
on the inside of his cheek, backing him off, cut blood in his mouth.

Allowed, in recompense, into the master's house where soft children
push chicken hearts at the ends of sticks into fire, their juices in his gullet,
he rests, is well fed and warm. He will perform for them his huckaback trick,

jumping into the air and slamming his behind into the door to peals of giggles.
One sweetness placed a mantilla on his head and to singing and to dancing
drew him through their rooms at the end of a shiny purple ribbon.

Winter Gigue

In preparation for this season's monster blizzard,
snowflakes are falling. The old woman who wraps her legs
and pocketbook in cellophane has slipped, the season's

first casualty. There are dogs of many breeds: beribboned
maltese; waddling pekingese with gold coat and fat feet;
appalled poodle, coiffed; hulking newfoundland in need of grooming…

In the high-windowed studio, the ballet mistress strikes a future
of fear and awe: *Plié is the first thing you learn, and the last
thing you master.* In snow-white leotards, thin little girls begin.

Divertissement

Even if I stuff the entrance to my ears
With cotton, my hands, the flaps of my thick wool cap,
Ophelia just won't stop singing. Whirling
In circles on bare, still vigorous feet,
Like a shabby goddess from a traveling
Circus where the elephant, prodded with a stick,
Is made to lift its gargantuan leg,
And the glacial acrobats in green culottes
Go round and round on the sway
Of a huge brown horse, the vaunted coloratura
Keeps coming, opening up her chest
And offering up her breath with every measure:
Famed Purgatory Aria, all scales and never solace.

Muses

The Muses are giving a thousand poets, painters, dancers
The back of their hands, and having flown, seat themselves
On the hypnotically spinning stools of Hartley Farms
Where they are mouthing the giant menu with tremendous glee:
Raspberry swirl, chocolate marshmallow fudge, swiss mocha almond…
And motioning for Marina and Sophia in their green-and-white aprons
With fictive cows grazing, and leaning over the counter on alabaster arms,
Whispering, "Girls, do not despair, ever, for we are here," so that the tired
Servers swipe their dark, perspired hair from their faces and wonder
Who is speaking, who is near and what in the world is forever.

Asbury Park

Themis, Greek reader of tea leaves, peers out from her white booth on the boardwalk, after a morning of tense, blank clients.

You will marry an engineer…
You will have beautiful children with long gold hair…

The dirty ocean is rough. Seagulls flock and squawk maniacally.

You will voyage to faraway lands of opulent palaces and friendly roosters…
You will open your screen door and find a cat who will save your life…

They want a piece of fish the way the mumbling drunk on the bench wants a piece of ass.

Your child will discover a cure for cancer, his face on a postage stamp…

A solemn boy in a crisp white shirt brings a miniature violin to his chin. His spellbound bow, his hypnotized eyes!

You will live to a ripe old age and fall in love with leaves as you once did…

Art Brut

Judith Scott, in memoriam (1943-2005)

Her bundled woebegones,
Her sheltered primevals,
With a stapler lodged in the brain,
Torso stuffed with a corkscrew,
Sister's lost car keys, child's left shoe,
Or bits of foam, pages from a book,
And the broken back of a chair.
Give up all hope for a better past.
Judy pulls the living from the dead
And whatever is at her slippered feet,
Within her ravenous, flower-girl grasp—
The process is unstoppable,
The process is humming.

Figure with Hat
James Castle (1899-1977), Outsider Artist

Face split in two, the stake of black soot and spit

running up and down the body. Nothing but the grit

it takes to keep going in this life, the lonely pitch,

the Christ on his raw wood, the undertaker in his stiff

black suit…Earthen as Idaho, mute, Castle scowls.

He'll show his drawings to kin across the way and if

they laugh, to hell with them. Nothing to see here,

missy. You're kidding yourself if you think there is.

The Cellar

Under the locked grille, the animals are crying.

You hear them while you wait and when the bus pulls up,

Finally, and you get on. That was years ago. The cellar

Is given over to new shopkeepers, one after the other,

Who fail and are replaced. Even the selfish brother,

The crazed neighbor, the criminal in his cell, face of blue

Tattoos, has never allowed a living thing to starve

As you have. Who knows this except for you and the laughing

African with his padlock teeth and flashing gold key.

On Forgetting

Make us real, make us lasting.
We will sit like Theseus on our chairs of snow,
Fading without complaint like the chalk on the arm
Of the tailor's dress, our blood on the sheets.
To be ravenous again! The mouth, the eyes must open wide,
The air to rush in again.
Grant us a second chance, a third…
In this palace of marble and onyx,
Even the ice is old and tired. Her brown hair,
Burnished by the mountain's breeze,
Her shoulder braids tied by red dusty rods,
And the warm earth below on the first days of Spring—
Beauty without exaggeration.

IV

Hostage
for W.S. Merwin

God is in the dogs
The one who turns in circles, the one
With scabs, the one who wears the collar
Who stares and stares
And tries in spite of it to smell the dirt and grass
In the abandonment, torrential muteness
My knees loosened, my glassy eyes of crystals warmed
And it was given
Even should we sleep
Turn weep recite, screaming, "the city is conquered and the little king
Will have to go," insane and unreachable
We are still here

An Old Illness

Little gargoyles cup their ears the better
to hear the breath go shallow: a gentle wind,

so as not to kick up the trees, not to knock
down the house. No one knows but *you*,

they whisper in smoky voices. Mortal without
future, spleen or example, you are coming apart!

The limbs, eyes, heart are like a river drying up;
the land dying out and all its threadbare wanderers,

fly-infested, the universe strapped to their backs,
are leading their goats and camels over the hill.

Elsewhere green reigns like fat Henry, water's
in the well and even the rheumy dog is hankering

after the fluttering pigeons. Hey, human, you
have made all the choices you are going to make.

Notre Dame de Paris

What gusts of raw, mad emotion, of unbearable expectation, in this world-cutting-loose of the bells. A crucifix, fashioned of twigs, is being held up to all the draculas, who, convulsed, are going up in smoke to a shriek. Quaking birds are calling for assembly and their plaintive crying is being carried over the voice of the gun. Now the dead are stepping out of their wet shoes, and loosened from their withered chords, are calling to us from the deck of their boat: *Bon voyage, mes chers!* We are beside ourselves: *in ekstasis!*

LAZARUS, COME OUT

The sisters are wailing, quite beside themselves with something new.
The pale Christ, lanky as a long-distance runner, seems half-amazed
at what he has done. Sitting up, the awakened one sees the immobile

face of the woman he mounted like a maniac, his body erupting in fever,
in abscess, for want of her, and is indifferent. He can hear the murmurs,
the jeers and coarse laughter on the roads and in the homes, the crush

of a slapped face, the unhinged bells, the dangerous, sullen gaps.
Suddenly visible are the closed faces of the doomers and the open faces
of the doomed, although he is a dark room, his tongue black and stiff.

Fanatics who worship the sun sever their arms as offerings
to help it rise; it rises, and the disinterred one, for a time, continues,
dancing by himself like a horse with its screaming, high-tossing head.

Anacreon

To close his eyes and metamorphose into a sleek wall of mirror

So that she might look at him; or into a satin dress to flow over the curves

Of her torso like a hand; or into a scented crème of white pears to be rubbed

Into her back; or into warm water to wash her feet and arms with, to sweeten

Her hair; or into a velvet braid or pearl necklace to tie round her throat

To graze at her breasts; or into a shoe so that she might push into him…

Old Anacreon, who choked to death on a grape, his waxen

Flesh scarcely able to remember that once it was suicidal, feverish,

And whose desires were as boundless as the night, as boundless.

Suzanne Farrell, *Davidsbündlertänze*

Instill in me a quieter walk, a calm face
for smiling. In your temple's silver pool,
the gentle swans are tucking their heads

into a bliss of down. The deer recede to dim-lit rooms.
Unknown unknowns await: the night will take
the mother with her Chinese-silver hair,

the child with a crooked eye, the golden cat,
whose vanishings, like deep music, only you
can hear, your long, smooth body bending.

Hibernation

Held together with glue, pins and a steel bolt of lightning,
I cede the world to two black bugs with tiny heads,
Bobbing and feasting on the kitchen table's cake crumbs.

Gorge to your bellies' content; weave and dance
                                          to your limbs' collapse
At this impromptu *Carnaval* of the Arthropods.

A light drizzle on the streets, on this holiday
To honor mothers, keeps us indoors, on our wooden chairs,
Arms laden with roses.

Metanoia

With a silent cockatoo on your bony shoulder, and turrets
on a cheap crown rusting, you are all wrong; and your dirty
heart can be hauled away in a red plastic bag, labeled hazardous,
labeled waste. Let something else be sewn in its place. Light as
a feather on naked feet you may dance and make stalks rise; delight
like the idiot for bald heads and sinuous fish under the heavy oceans;
adore like he who curls up inside her cameo with a sachet of lavender,
a little fog, a little fugue for company. Where you had no life, you will
be given life. Birds will take wing in jubilation, shy animals emerge
from the forest to catch a glimpse of you, and you will hear yourself saying,
like the old maid you once tortured: *You cannot imagine, it is not
Human nature to imagine what a nice walk we have round the Orchard.*

Middle World

Kneading her paws into the white blanket, my Penelope's eyes
Roll hysterically back into her delicate head,
And for one vacant moment she is unconcerned with hunger
And fright; with calculating love and cold, impenetrable
Loss. If she were a human, she'd be tying off
Her arm, blasted with a belt, and self-
Starved, tongue-warmed, be running slowly,
Quietly, along the steep banks of Lethe.

God of Sleep

The silent herd is standing in tall grass,
The wind is blowing hard, the axe is smashing through
The thickly iced-over trough. Each evening, benevolent

Clockwork, Morpheus leans close to Hypnos,
Pleading, "Father, close their tired eyes."

To Balanchine

The seraphim spot you, arms splayed, eyes swollen shut,

And send the white-robed ship to find you, the walls of wave,

By their approach, nearly drowning you—sad irony for having survived

So long a frightening distance from land. Now join your suffering

To ours, chime the delirious muses, and make for us the great dance.

Mixed beings of air, earth and water with voices like wild laughter

Whose faces you will never see, so covered are they by wings.

[EXIT, PURSUED BY A BEAR.

The callous henchman is the one devoured, the baby saved.
The wind picks up and sends the lazy dove-sails flying over waves

without a finger raised. Even the starved mongrel, abandoned
by your brother, pries open the ash can with its dirty snout

and finds a roasted chicken sitting right on top. Old-timers, every limb
aching to be straightened, march like pins. The torn angels are being fitted

for new gowns by the seamstress with cold lips. Turn, she mumbles. Turn,
the lovelies. The sun is granting her people a golden day, for no earthly reason.

CHERNOBYL

Crossing in the wrong direction, we are quickly

Sealed off, directionless, earth's blind villagers.

We follow the leader and the riverbank to its dried-out

Roots, while at the merest ruffle of wind, bird, leaf,

We hide ourselves behind the thick bodies of old trees

That have the tiny, sad eyes and the long, delicate lashes

Of chained elephants. We witness the quiet lives

Of fireflies, igniting themselves, their enviable wings;

The languorous butterfly climbing into the flower's face;

And begin to be muted by our arrival at the inconceivable

Door as when the radiated wolves crept into the hunters'

Huts to be comforted and were comforted.

Selected Poems from

Little Savage

A Note on Emily Fragos's *Little Savage*

You are alone in the room, reading her poems. Nothing is happening, nothing *wrong*, but all at once, say around page 17 or 18, you hear—remember, no one is with you, no one else there—a sigh. Or a whispered word: *someone.* You are not alarmed, but you had thought you were alone. Perhaps not. The sensation is what Freud used to call *unheimlich*, uncanny.

That is the effect of the poems of Emily Fragos. Like their maker, her readers are *accompanied*, and not to their ulterior knowledge. It is not disagreeable to be thus escorted, attended, *joined*, but we had not expected it. And as Robert Frost used to tell us ("no surprise in the writer, no surprise in the reader"), Fragos too has not expected such visitations, as she will call them. This poet—these poems—endure *otherness*, they are haunted:

> "I remain, with one of everything." "Even as one is being saved… conjure the army of others." "What would happen to my life when all along there has been nothing but me?" "Did you not see how I was made to feel when you put me among others?" "And my body—uninhabited—suffers and wonders: whose hands are these? whose hair?"

The poems will reveal whose, though I do not think Emily Fragos herself ever finds out. Inevitably, we recall that old surrealist shibboleth, "Tell me by what you are haunted and I will tell you who you are"; it can be the password to identity. But this poet has what she calls "luxurious mind" and her ghosts are legion:

> Alone in my odd-shaped room, I practice
> blindness and the world floats
> close and away. I am uncertain of
> everything. I must walk slowly, carefully.

She is acknowledging, with some uneasiness ("will you please tidy up?"), that it is not only the beloved dead, the proximate departed who are *with* her, who possess her, but others, *any others*. The remarkable thing about this poetic consciousness is that the woman's body is inhabited—sometimes with mere habitude, sometimes joyously, more often with astonishing pain—by the prolixity of the real (and of the 'unreal'); the poems are instinct with *others*:

> How dare you
> care for me when all my life
> I have had this voltage to ignite
> me, this rhythm to drive me,
> when something inside your body
> dares me to touch my hands
> to yours…

And quite as remarkable, of course, is the even tonality of such possession; there is nothing hysterical or even driven about the voice of the poems as it records, as it laments or exults in these unsought attendants. There is merely—merely!—a loving consistency of heedfulness; and one remembers Blake's beautiful aphorism: *unmixed attention is prayer.*

Of course such poetic staffage is not peculiar to Emily Fragos; like Maeterlinck, like Rilke, she exults in her discovered awareness: "I need the other/the way a virus/needs a host." Rather, she imbues, she *infects* all of us with the consciousness that there are no single souls: we are not alone.

Richard Howard

Little Savage

Apollo's Kiss

Devise Cassandra. Become her, in possession,
And the world becomes perfect. For even gods
Crave perfection. Desire her like a man
And like a man be refused in all your desire.
Surrender: beg a first and last kiss and pray
She will acquiesce, her virtue stirred.
Then, breathe into her mouth the powered
Prophesy and for all you are losing
—the deprivation she will give and give—
Release her half gifted, as you are, half mortal.

In the courtyard, animals are captured
By their hind legs, held up on haunches,
Throats slashed. She walks on burning
Stones. Swift, it is slaughtering season.

Mondays

Every village has its lunatic,
its talking parrot, its spot in the park
where lovers lie between two trees.

At the post office,
there she is, pushing her carriage
filled with garbage, her head a poodle
of ludicrous yellow curls.

She tells her Bengali doctor:
I don't know how long
it's been out there on the lawn,
but it's not dead yet.

He looks back at her
with liquid eyes
and speaks in spurts,
which makes her nervous,
makes her want to open
her mouth, sing opera.

She rushes from the clinic,
through the park, sees
the lovers sitting up, the round red blossoms,
the ink-black blossoms.

At the veterinarian's, the parrot
is being handed over for lung surgery
and calls out: *Come here.*
I love you. I want to go home.

Medieval

There was only a thin strip
of fantasy. I traced its patterns
in my bare feet, my gypsy bracelets
clicking at my wrists. It never
wore out—you on one end—
a body in blue adagio.

The cords reminded me of everything
sensual I loved. Now the cello
is put back in its huge human
case and stands voiceless
against the bedroom wall.

Tomorrow I will cart it
downstairs into the streets
filled with the curses of plague.
The children will throw stones.
The bronze bell will sound.

Tomorrow I will carry you
downstairs into the clutter
for the festive insane to sleep inside.

Glenn Gould, Dead at 50

It is darker where I am.
I cannot tell, holding my hand
over one eye, if it is female there.

At six,
I multiplied endlessly
and began to feel close
to sacrifice.

The music took root
inside, like torture,
all tension, ritard, release.

It is in every part
of my body now, and there is not
room left for me.

I have burned
all my capes, got rid of my papers.

GRACES

Your son gives you a ring to wear and you wear it.
Thalia and Melpomene, identical masks with inverted mouths,
the little faces on your fourth finger you stare at

when he is gone and you mourn, moving about the rooms
of your expensive home in a bruise, touching your fingers
to his shoes, his clothes, his hairbrush on the bureau.

It is rude to leave messages that do not get answered,
your friends tell you. Walking about like a ghoul, they say.
They crush you with their extravagance for grief has made you
simple and one glance: *But this has nothing to do with manners.*

I imagine you turning a corner, a bag slung over your shoulder,
rushing to meet him at the door of the schoolhouse
and only this matters: the metal ring on your finger,
raising matching cups to your lips in soothing synchrony.

The Art of the Insane

The good Doctor Prinzhorn says it was the patent
that snapped me in two like a twig,
that shattered my lovely personality, so to speak.
I nod my heavy head.

Have you seen my machine, perpetually moving,
whirring, breathing? Made it out of cloth
and mud and dirt and spit and excrement.

Dear Diary: Dubuffet and Klee came last week
to copy my faces. Eager to meet me, touching
my creatures with their long, skinny fingers.

They smeared my orange chalk, calculating
what they could steal . . . . And if anyone asks,

I am taking my pig Rafi for a walk.
With her hooves of long curls like a little girl's
mop, or Persian slippers, excellent for flying,

we are wind gone. We are kingdom come.

Logic

I started smoking again after a long time
without. I don't remember why I lit up:

some envy, some fear I could not face. Went
to the corner and bought my brand and took it

up so easily in my hand, my mouth, I could
not imagine not ever performing this fluid

motion. It tasted bitter and my head
was dizzy but I kept at it until it changed

to smooth forgetfulness and warmth filled
my lungs. Fresh air was slim and common

compared to this, beautiful darkness.
And gone the enormity of quitting, how it was

suddenly always this powerless sweet hunger
so strong I wondered how I never ended up

with needle marks in some shooting gallery,
with dirty clothes and dirty hair, some

mountain-heavy man on top of me. It was
easier to imagine than me on some campus

with books in my arms taking notes with
a black felt-tip pen. Now I am up to two

packs a day. I can feel my body collapsing
as I walk the streets. I can feel people

staring at me, uncovering all my secrets
in broad daylight. Eventually I will have

to start thinking about stopping all over
again. And keep in mind this time what they

always say: Watch out for false highs;
there is another person with your eyes,

hair, and mouth on the other side of the room
whispering *hurt thyself, starve,* and it

will seem the perfectly right thing to do.

Visitations, But None Come

Flightless bird
ravenous on dust
for sustenance.

Little savage
taking its revenge at will
with stopped-up mouth.

Ugly feet
pick up dry sticks
like poems

pen clenched
between prehensile toes.

Host

There are two worlds I know of:
the vast illumined
and the place where I am.

I need the other
the way a virus
needs a host,
but the strange,
loving sisters
hold up their hands.

And my body—
uninhabited—
suffers and wonders:
Whose hands are these?
Whose hair?

While You Slept

The crows, with soft, astonished flush,
lift from their branches, as no living thing without wings

can get about. There was a great fire
in the city while you slept: fire engines, hoses,

torrential gushes of water looped through open
smoking windows. From the roof, screams and hands

reaching up and down. Ladders all the way to heaven
as one at a time bodies were lowered and others

remained. Someone hurled himself like a mounted acrobat
from a ledge into the empty air. Sirens wailed in the distance.

Cri de Coeur

What if you said yes
to everything. What would happen
to me then. I am telling you
the rage would start and never
come to end. How dare you
care for me when all my life
I have had this voltage to ignite
me, this rhythm to drive me,
when something inside your body
dares me to touch my hands
to yours. And if you said go
ahead, touch. What would happen
to my life then, when all along
there has been nothing but me.

The Path

There is so little to go on: a pale
trembling hand as I stand over you,
my finger tracing the words on the page,
a foreign language you are learning
for a journey without me. You will do
fine, I say. You will wrap your tongue
around these sounds and be understood,
be given what you desire: a loaf of bread,
change for your money, an antique doll
with violent eyes. Paintings are hanging
on walls, behind glass, waiting for you
to admire them. Their plaintive beauty
will move through you and you will walk
back to your hotel through the park
I know well. I spent years there walking
its bridle path, a gray cat in my arms,
moving toward you, blind, in another life.

The Drowned

Even as one is being saved, pulled by the sopping collar
from an ivory ocean, limbs quivering, and bundled

by sturdy hands in green blankets, conjure the army of others,
having fallen out of rocking boats, having swum

too far, after the sudden ankle-pull under, after the astonished
plunge, the soft twig-crack of extinction—how solemnly

they drift away. And even as the rescued one, frigid hands
rubbed pink, air bursting like lilac sachets in the lungs,

is roused to land, a foreign feeling in the legs,
they open and shut their mouths like sullen fish,

making precise, pathetic gestures with their frozen figures,
going deeper and out farther, even as through a pond's

diaphanous patch, a gloved hand hovers to remove another,
skates still laced at the feet, from their mute presence,

moving still behind closed, curved eyes, inside strange skin.

Company

I've lost my stately others and now there is me with neck
erect and solemn, tightened face. Sometimes I feel they are
peering out from behind white curtains, clutching with long

arthritic fingers the edges of chenille, wiping their mouths
as after a succulent roast or giggling like ninnies in the pantry.
Once I turned, but it was only a wisp of my own dark hair.

I wanted them gone for so long, world devised of nothing
but me, distractionless, pure, but I was wrong. Me is empty
as wilderness, air—no monarchs, no moths.

In the Egyptian Museum

The light and taunting voice, so filled with wild embellishment,
grows heavy, without shine, and sinks to the bottom of the pool.

Trees behind long windows stare in—somber, disciplined—
old women with gnarl in their bones and a patience for clouds

and the sullen glares of the malcontent. The deaf schoolchildren
pick at their lips and sit on marble benches, waiting to be led home

by the hot hand, up narrow steps, and lifting their scented dresses
above their heads, slip quietness on, as devotion commands.

In Memoriam

What lives in the dark humming—not symphony, not divinity,
not the author of her life. It is cooing to her as Othello
coos to Desdemona—as the bawdy nurse to her pretty Susan.

Behind her lies the city in silver and blue sliver. No one sails
on the river of myth; no one holds her breath. A wild bird
is preparing with utmost concentration for its next move,

which will not take place for one million years.
And the spiders, picked up and dropped at will by a gust,
leave their legs behind to dance in the air, spinning on a grief.

Sorrow

She is small-boned and shy, offends us by her silence.
We wish to make her real until she arrives like a guest
and won't pack her foul-smelling clothes or stop stealing

our cherished possessions. The candelabra went first,
smashed to crystal bits in a childish fit of rage, a snit
because we happened to be out of peanut butter. She put

the pet ferret's tiny tail in the rat trap in back of the fridge
and totaled our new Toyota. On Saturday night, sorrow's
robed in a cranberry dress and sports a huge gold buckle

at the belted waist. She draws compliments all around
for her upswept hair and false lashes, her large anemone
eyes set wide apart, and the high forehead, a sign

of intelligence. She folds her legs at the lovely knees.
My mother and sister are arriving for Christmas, sorrow
squeals. Sorrow has a sister! Put the cat on top of the tree

instead of the star, the sorrow-child laughs, and how like
our unlike mothers we emerge to become. Sorrow hasn't
brushed her teeth or hair in centuries. We put pen and paper

out for her to write letters with in the middle of the night.
This adds charm to my thoughts, she explains. Sorrow is so full
of herself. The snow saturates her body, cold as a radiator,

and "Can't you turn the heat up, cheapskates? I'm freezing!"
she screeches from the attic, where she goes to dance. Long
after we are in our beds, tired heads upon the world's pillows,

you can hear the thumping and pounding of her long feet,
tapping at the ground like a palomino. The stalky elegance,
the pointy toes of sorrow. We have not slept in years.

Hall of Records

The birth occurred in the morning and the doctor's name
was Italian. There was no catastrophe of mindless proportion

in Quito, Ecuador, that buried thousands alive in a river of mud.
Neither was it boiling out but simply mild, for you have checked

the newspaper's headlines for that day. The president
did not call in the troops to keep peace among the rioting looters.

The police never did catch that murderer who left the girl
child behind the schoolhouse, one shoe off and never found:

a trophy he retains in an old trunk stowed under his bed.
At night he takes them out—left shoe, charm bracelet, barrette—

to touch and smell. His name is not John. The two brown horses
tethered to the riding pole were grazing in the field when the boy,

dreaming of Sarah, threw his smoke into the stall and walked away.
He did not hear the horses stirring, did not write a bad love song,

practicing three chords on a cheap guitar well into the night.
There is no Sarah. A woman once again on that day failed to call

the boiler repairman; he never took the toothpick from his mouth
to fix her eyeglasses with, where the little pin had fallen out.

Increase of Appetite

Scrawny and pallid creatures taken pity on and bought
from the store while the chartreuse and royal-blue parakeets

had to be left behind; but then, the guilt of having left them
prompted a renewed excursion to other stores and other birds:

parrots with torn feathers and cracked beaks, cockatoos turning
grim yellow at the chin, even pigeons, standing frozen on the city

sidewalks, carried home half dead inside newspapers while riding
on crowded buses and kept in shoe boxes on the bathroom floor

until they died inside. (I bury them in the park at night. There are
ordinances against it.) My life is not my own. I spend my time

feeding them, scooping out seed of one kind or another, vitamins,
antibiotics, with little bird spoons and replacing their bowls of water

and cleaning up after them. I put covers over their cages but you
don't know owls with their rotating heads and nightingales that sing

in the dark—lovely music but not lulling really. Not satisfying,
not compatible in a human way. Most mad-screech and
    nasal-whine,

blurting out *peter peter* or *phoebe phoebe* all hours of the day.
They become despondent and won't leave their cages, looking
    out at me

as if to say, *But what is my crime, sir, that you keep me here?* Now that
people hear the cacophony, they give me theirs or what they find,

but what do they do but overwhelm one who is already
    overwhelmed!
You do not know. They have their own rules and deaths
    and routes

to follow—there above the darkening trees, there along
    the hushed river,
there where no one yet has traced them to an Andean
    mountaintop

like the Monarchs all gold and black and silently drumming.
If the food runs out, if the winter cold freezes them to the hollow,

if there are those who fall behind or drift from the pattern from
    weakness
or bad eyesight, the perils of predation, and fall away,
    irretrievable—

A million sorries I say to the birds; a million sorries they sing
    back to me.

The Scarlatti Sun

The mute seamstress on her knees
sticks a pin in the hem
and weeps for the cloth;

the dead stop their dying,
their heads warming like stones
in the Scarlatti sun,

while the grave postman,
his worn leather bag strapped to his back,
feels his mind go, windswept.

An old woman at her window,
her old cat on the sill, sips thick coffee
from a saucer, and in the shuttered convent,

the novitiate, taken up,
rushes across the just-washed floor,
daring the ground to break a bone.

Notes

Page 23: "the little O, Earth" is a phrase by William Shakespeare.

Page 36: *Into Great Silence* is the title of a documentary film, directed by Philip Gröning.

Page 41: "for Kaspar Hauser" — Quote on line 6 is from the film, *The Enigma of Kaspar Hauser*, directed by Werner Herzog.

Page 42: *Winter Carnival in a Small Flemish Town* was painted by Peeter Gysels.

Page 43: "Quartet for the End of Time" is the title of a chamber music piece, composed by Olivier Messiaen.

Page 45: "Winter Gigue" — Quote on lines 8-9 is attributed to ballerina, Suzanne Farrell.

Page 62: "Metanoia" — Quote on lines 11-12 is from the *Letters of Jane Austen*.

Page 66: "*[Exit, pursued by a bear.*" is a famous stage direction from Shakespeare's *The Winter's Tale*.

The author wishes to thank her sister, Elizabeth Fragos Faranda, and her friends, Barbara Puro Rosenthal and Timothy Donnelly, for their sustaining support and assistance.

Thank you to Reiko Davis of Sheep Meadow Press for her excellent work on the manuscript. Finally, a special thank you to Stanley Moss for his gracious and generous support and for making this book possible.